Lizette Woodworth Reese

A Quiet Road

Lizette Woodworth Reese

A Quiet Road

ISBN/EAN: 9783744678292

Printed in Europe, USA, Canada, Australia, Japan

Cover: Foto ©Thomas Meinert / pixelio.de

More available books at **www.hansebooks.com**

A QUIET ROAD

The Riverside Press
Cambridge

A QUIET ROAD

BY

LIZETTE WOODWORTH REESE

BOSTON AND NEW YORK
HOUGHTON, MIFFLIN AND COMPANY
M DCCC XCVI

TO
SOPHIA LOUISA

THE ROAD OF REMEMBRANCE

The old wind stirs the hawthorn tree;
    The tree is blossoming;
Northward the road runs from the sea,
    And past the House of Spring.

The folk go down it unafraid;
    The still roofs rise before;
When you were lad and I was maid,
    Wide open stood that door.

Now, other children crowd the stair,
    And hunt from room to room;
Outside, under the hawthorn fair,
    We pluck the thorny bloom.

Out in the quiet road we stand,
    Shut in from wharf and mart,
The old wind blowing up the land,
    The old thoughts at our heart.

CONTENTS

AN ENGLISH MISSAL

UPON these pages clear,
I, Basil, write my name;
My task is ended, and the year
Is gone out like a flame.

Martin and John the good
Are gathered to the blest;
It seems an hour ago they stood
And praised me with the rest.

I missed them when they went;
Then filled this page with palms,
And saw them both — their travail spent —
Harbored in heavenly calms.

The tulips in this book,
Their like our garden knew;
All spring what could I do but look,
And set them here anew?

The saint that yonder walks
Smiles from our chancel space;
But Mary with the lily-stalks
Has mine own mother's face.

The thought of her was sweet
As blossoms are in Lent;
Green turned our winding convent street,
And all about was Kent.

Kent lilies round her nod;
I drew her staid and fair;
I drew her with the Son of God
Clasped to her bosom there.

Brief is our life and dark;
The grave shall hold us fast;
Yet find I here in old Saint Mark
That only right shall last.

I, Basil, too, must heed,
Else were my task undone.
God has more books than I can read;
I praise Him for this one.

A PASTORAL

OHO, my love, oho, my love, and ho,
    the bough that shows,
    Against the grayness of mid-Lent
    the color of the rose !
The lights o' Spring are in the sky and down
    among the grass ;
Bend low, bend low, ye Kentish reeds, and let
    two lovers pass !

The plum-tree is a straitened thing ; the cherry
    is but vain ;
The thorn but black and empty at the turning
    of the lane ;
Yet mile by mile out in the wind the peach-trees
    blow and blow,
And which is stem, and which is bloom, not
    any maid can know.

The ghostly ships sail up to town and past the
    orchard wall ;

There is a leaping in the reeds; they waver
    and they fall;
For lo, the gusts of God are out; the April
    time is brief;
The country is a pale red rose, and dropping
    leaf by leaf.

I do but keep me close beside, and hold my
    lover's hand;
Along the narrow track we pass across the
    level land;
The petals whirl about us and the sedge is to
    our knees;
The ghostly ships sail up, sail up, beyond the
    stripping trees.

When we are old, when we are cold, and
    barrèd is the door,
The memory of this will come and turn us
    young once more;
The lights o' Spring will dim the grass and
    tremble from the sky;
And all the Kentish reeds bend low to let us
    two go by!

CHARLES LAMB

LOVER of London, not a violet
    Purpled at a shop-door the end o'
        Lent,
    But thought he higher than all its
        kind in Kent;
And if the door were carved — then better yet !
Elizabethan laughter fills his time,
He heard it echoing and made it his ;
And with its smacking words for that or this,
He set to prose what others saved for rhyme.
Past cheat of years the comrades of his mood —
The quiet old men sitting in the sun ;
Strict maids ; gray clerks ; · and children fair
      and blest ;
And that sad woman of his house and blood —
And still he hides his hurts from dearest one ;
But with the whole world shares the stingless
      jest !

TELLING THE BEES

A COLONIAL CUSTOM

ATHSHEBA came out to the sun,
Out to our wallèd cherry-trees ;
The tears adown her cheek did run,
Bathsheba standing in the sun,
Telling the bees.

My mother had that moment died ;
Unknowing, sped I to the trees,
And plucked Bathsheba's hand aside ;
Then caught the name that there she cried
Telling the bees.

Her look I never can forget,
I that held sobbing to her knees;
The cherry-boughs above us met;
I think I see Bathsheba yet
Telling the bees.

HER LAST WORD

EMEMBER or forget me, as you
    will !
Keep me in mind, as one on the
    June's edge
Keeps the sole bloom that starred the sad
    March sedge,
Because it was the first, and hours were chill.
Or, else, let me be naught of good or ill;
The snow that one time whirled within the
    hedge;
Some fair, forgotten thing, too slight for pledge,
Vanished too long to make your pulses thrill:
When you do weep, my tears are salt as yours;
You laugh, and all my loads are light to bear;
Back of my sweetest thought a sweeter yet,
You bide with me, and will while life endures.
Let me remember; but if aught of care
Pricks you through me, then do you, love,
    forget !

IN TIME OF GRIEF

DARK, thinned, beside the wall of
    stone,
The box dripped in the air ;
Its odor through my house was
    blown
Into the chamber there.

Remote and yet distinct the scent,
The sole thing of the kind,
As though one spoke a word half meant
That left a sting behind.

I knew not Grief would go from me,
And naught of it be plain,
Except how keen the box can be
After a fall of rain.

LOVE CAME BACK AT FALL O' DEW

LOVE came back at fall o' dew,
Playing his old part;
But I had a word or two
That would break his heart.

"He who comes at candlelight,
That should come before,
Must betake him to the night
From a barrèd door."

This the word that made us part
In the fall o' dew;
This the word that brake his heart —
Yet it brake mine, too!

INDIAN SUMMER

CAST on this shore at end of year,
Survivors of the wreck and storm,
We build our fire of driftwood here,
Somewhat to gain of the old cheer,
And spread our stiffened hands to warm.
Nor gold nor any spice have we ;
From West or East no carvèd things ;
But ever to us keeps and clings
The stinging odor of the sea !

A STREET SCENE

THE east is a clear violet mass
    Behind the houses high ;
    The laborers with their kettles
        pass ;
The carts are creaking by.

Carved out against the tender sky,
    The convent gables lift ;
Half way below the old boughs lie
    Heaped in a great white drift.

They tremble in the passionate air ;
    They part, and clean and sweet
The cherry flakes fall here, fall there ;
    A handful stirs the street.

The workmen look up as they go ;
    And one, remembering plain
How white the Irish orchards blow,
    Turns back, and looks again.

WAITING FOR SONG

ALL my roads climb to you, and my
whole year
To days elect and few,
Thrust toward the spring-time, in
an atmosphere
Sifted of frost or dew;
Shut to Remembrance, Song, away from you.

More than Remembrance; Expectation here,
Beside that other set,
Waits in this tender season.   Draw you near
Swift as the violet?
God answers me with you: I have you yet.

At root of crocus; at the heart of tree;
And in the shower's drip;
Fleeting like wind the hollow dusks for me;
Back to my best I slip,
Remembering you: I run, but you outstrip.

Grown used to Spring, oh, I shall understand;
No strange thing will it be,
To watch it surge in billows up the land!
Grown used to you, to see
You rising up, come back from God to me!

ROBERT LOUIS STEVENSON

I N his old gusty garden of the North,
He heard lark-time the uplifting
Voices call;
Smitten through with Voices was
the evenfall —
At last they drove him forth.

Now there were two rang silverly and long;
And of Romance, that spirit of the sun,
And of Romance, spirit of youth, was one;
And one was that of Song.

Gold-belted sailors, bristling buccaneers,
The flashing soldier, and the high, slim dame,
These were the Shapes that all around him
came, —
That we let go with tears.

His was the unstinted English of the Scot,
Clear, nimble, with the scriptural tang of Knox

Thrust through it like the far, strict scent of
     box,
To keep it unforgot.

No frugal Realist, but quick to laugh,
To see appealing things in all he knew,
He plucked the sun-sweet corn his fathers
     grew,
And would have naught of chaff.

David and Keats, and all good singing men,
Take to your hearts this Covenanter's son,
Gone in mid-years, leaving our years undone,
Where you do sing again!

AUTUMN TO SPRING

OF the emptying hands but the
quick heart,
I, that was Spring, to me
Troop gust-like Visions where I
muse apart;
From days long-gone I see
Oncoming days, O Spring that is to be!

I, the gray Reaper, putting life aside
As an engathered sheaf,
Recall the furrows and the lost seed-tide,
The tumult sweet and brief
That shakes the land into the curlèd leaf.

Lo, that white handful at the orchard's door!
Spent with remembering,
I long for some poor sign of places hoar,
And straight that ghostly thing
As token that I once was Sower and Spring.

Ecstatic hours; the pangs of growth, its fires,
Its sudden, stormy calls,
Are yours; the immemorial desires;
The spectral mood that falls
Along with dusk by broken pasture-walls.

Yet ever is the old at root of new;
Across your slender grass
My foot shall sound; back of each thought of
        you
Be that of Hallowmas;
The Long Since as a shadow come and pass.

Then shall you be, O Spring, like unto him
Who bides, young heir of all,
In an old house, with many memories dim,
Engirt by poplars tall,
And knows not why his tears begin to fall.

He hears without the delicate winds go by,
And one thrush twilightward,
Loosing his heart unto the quiet sky;
But indoors sits he, pored
Over vague tales of the dear, vanished lord.

Upon your jocund face that look I bear
Shall as a seal be set;
Folk will remember; one shall fieldward fare
Under the hedges wet,
And find my dead leaves round your violet.

A WHITE LILAC

I KNOW you ghost of some lone,
    delicate hour,
  Long-gone but unforgot;
Wherein I had for guerdon and
    for dower
  That one thing I have not.

Unplucked I leave your mystical white feather,
  O phantom up the lane;
For back may come that spent and lovely
    weather,
  And I be glad again!

TO A TOWN POET

SNATCH the departing mood ;
　　Make yours its emptying reed, and
　　　　pipe us still
　　Faith in the time, faith in our
　　　　common blood,
Faith in the least of good ;
Song cannot fail if these its spirit fill !

What if your heritage be
The huddled trees along the smoky ways ;
At a street's end the stretch of lilac sea ;
The vender, swart but free,
Crying his yellow wares across the haze ?

Your verse awaits you there ;
For Love is Love though Latin swords be rust ;
The keen Greek driven from gossiping mall
　　　　and square ;
And Care is still but Care
Though Homer and his seven towns are dust.

Thus Beauty lasts, and, lo!
Now Proserpine is barred from Enna's hills,
The flower she plucked yet makes an April
show,
Sets some town sill a-glow,
And yours the Vision of the Daffodils.

The Old-World folk knew not
More surge-like sounds than urban winters
bring
Up from the wharves at dusk to every spot;
And no Sicilian plot
More fire than heaps our tulips in the spring.

Strait is the road of Song,
And they that be the last are oft the first;
Fret not for fame; the years are kind though
long;
You, in the teasing throng,
May take all time with one shrewd lyric burst.

Be reverend and know
Ill shall not last, or waste the ploughèd land;

Or creeds sting timid souls ; and naught at all,
Whatever else befall,
Can keep us from the hollow of God's hand.

Let trick of words be past ;
Strict with the thought, unfearful of the form,
So shall you find the way and hold it fast,
The world hear, at the last,
The horns of morning sound above the storm.

A CRICKET IN AUTUMN

H Shape, beyond the orchard pal-
                ings there,
        What moods of memory holds this
                lessening light,
The lilac, fading sky, or, crooked and white,
The young moon set above the plum-trees bare?
For these do in your music have a share.
But, under all, your one thin, antique note,
Past youth and time, and evermore remote,
As from the world's rim cuts the autumn air.
Certain am I that Song is not in vain ;
And yet, despite your piping, come and pass
The phantom chords of him that to our door
Brought laughter like sweet gusts that follow
        rain.
His reed lies snapped and rotting in the
        grass :
Yours, too, shall fail and you be heard no more !

WRIT IN A BOOK OF ELIZABETHAN VERSE

NCOMING Hour of light and dew,
Of heartier sun, more certain blue,
My shadow on your face doth fall.
I am the first sweet thing of all ;
By that much the more sweet than you.

Mine is the crocus and the call
Of gust to gust in shrubberies tall ;
The white tumult, the rainy hush ;
And mine the unforgetting thrush
That pours its heart-break from the wall.

For I am Tears, for I am Spring,
The old and immemorial thing ;
To me come ghosts by twos and threes,
Under the swaying cherry-trees,
From east and west remembering.

O elder Hour, when I am not,
Gone out like smoke from road and plot,
More perfect Hour of light and dew,
Shall lovers turn away from you,
And long for me, the Unforgot!

AN OLD BELLE

A DAUGHTER of the Cavaliers
  (A phrase a little dulled with
      years),
But something sweeter than them
    all,
Serene she sits at evenfall.

Tall tulips crowd the window-sill,
Vague ghosts of those that blew at will —
Ere she was old and time so fleet —
In one walled space down Camden street.

And straight — she and her lover there —
In that town garden take the air;
Tall tulips lift in scarlet tire,
Brimming the April dusk with fire.

Without, the white of harbored ships;
The road that to the water slips;

The tang of salt; the scent of sea;
Within, her only love and she!

Back to the new she comes once more,
To roofs ungabled, ways that roar;
To the sole April left her still,
That potted scarlet on the sill.

Dust are those pleasant garden walls;
Her only love in green Saint Paul's;
Serene she sits at her day's close;
Last of her kin, but still a rose!

THE SHEPHERD

ACROSS the Park, at set of sun,
   The shepherd drives his sheep;
The little lambs that scarce can run
   But by their mothers keep.

The town roars on without the gate;
   There comes a wavering gust
Of children's laughter, and the grate
   Of wheels along the dust.

A figure scriptural and kind,
   Cut out against the brass
That deepens in the west behind,
   He follows through the grass.

He gives a Syrian look to things,
   From highest unto least;
To sky, to beechen bough, there clings
   A flavor of the East.

With hurrying noises close but light
   Straight to the fold they keep ;
A pastoral spread before our sight,
   A shepherd and his sheep.

.

A FORGOTTEN ANCESTOR

IS fathers all were clerkly men,
    (Or so he has been told);
They loved a gossip now and then,
    The town ways shrewd and bold.

They hang — each in a carvèd frame —
    Along the dusky stair;
Thence can he see at thick o' spring
    The lilacs in the square.

His the colonial parson's eyes;
    The dash of cavalier;
And his the brow of him who lies
    Dust in old Warwickshire.

He sees the lilacs in the square,
    Purple, hazy, and slim;
The portraits fade from out the stair;
    The town itself is dim.

For when the April chills and thrills,
One moment rude and deep,
He climbs the everlasting hills,
A shepherd with his sheep !

THE DAY BEFORE SPRING

THERE is a faltering crimson by the
    wall,
    Now on a vine, and now on
      brier thinned,
As though one bearing lantern through the
    wind,
Here hides his light, but yonder lets it fall.
And we remember and remember ; all
    Ancestral stirrings point unto this fate, —
    That we shall come unto our old estate,
Defrauding days unloose their iron thrall.
Without, the trees seem crowding to the street,
    Like simple folk that breathless here and
      there
    Crowd toward a haunted space, to verify
Some dim report of ghost or vision fleet ;
    And lo, at dusk, across the silent square,
      As in a whirl of bloom, a Shape goes by !

IN HARBOR

I F hungry, Lord, I need but bread ;
  If I be faint, a cooling cup ;
  Naught, if I weary, save a bed ;
  If halt, a staff to hold me up ;
If needy, fields to till :
Yet, Lord, I wait Thy will.

HERRICK

H, Herrick, still we love you, and
       our days
       Keep to the weather of the daffodil,
       Because, good Mayer, your few
           notes do still
Break with their silver down our sullen ways.
Last of your line that knew to clearly sing,
You kept your heart up to the bloomy time,
Spending your Devon in unvexèd rhyme,
And with no mood except that one of Spring.
Oh, still we come, — as to some fair estate,
Which should be theirs, yet somehow is not so,
Come poor and wistful heirs from overseas,
To long and look without the fast-barred
       gate — .
And track you by your laughter where you go
At thick of morn under the rectory trees!

TRUST

I AM Thy grass, O Lord!
    I grow up sweet and tall
But for a day; beneath Thy sword
    To lie at evenfall.

Yet have I not enough
    In that brief day of mine?
The wind, the bees, the wholesome stuff
    The sun pours out like wine.

Behold, this is my crown;
    Love will not let me be;
Love holds me here; Love cuts me down;
    And it is well with me.

Lord, Love, keep it but so;
    Thy purpose is full plain;
I die that after I may grow
    As tall, as sweet again.

INSPIRATION

UPON the hills I left my sheep;
 Shepherd no more was I,
 With staff and scrip a watch to
  keep;
My flocks were of the sky.

I ran down to the river-reeds;
 I set the foremost loose;
I made it ready for my needs,
 And sweet enough for use.

The rude East smote me where I stood;
 The stars were great and few;
Sudden, along the expectant wood,
 A wavering note I blew.

Fog wrapped me in a winding-sheet;
 Nor sky nor road was clear;
I blew a note so echoing sweet
 The night rose up to hear.

The kine came from the pastures chill ;
  The flock came from the fold ;
By tavern-sides the folk sat still ;
  The dead stirred in the mould.

Ere yet the dark was at its close,
  Quaking I blew once more ;
The silence petaled like a rose,
  And all my song was o'er.

Myriad and golden past the wood,
  The spears of morn grew plain ;
Empty within the light I stood
  And brake my reed in twain.

THE THRUSH IN THE ORCHARD

N the edge of the close,
    Oh my heart, and my heart, do
        you hear
The song of that thrush?
The west it is like to a rose,
And the low white trees in the hush
Stand up in the quick of the year,
Oh my heart, in the quick of the year!

Round and black is the pool,
Out of ivory carved in the lane;
A shadowy thing
The house in its garden so cool,
In the lilac haze of the spring,
Its chimneys but ancient and vain;
Yet the song, oh the song, is full plain!

April comes to his own,
But he hears in the grass, as he goes,

The Aprils that were;
Before him, behind him, are blown
Dim sounds through the hush and the stir;
Both Loss and Possession he knows,
And the song sings them both in the close.

Delicate, rich, and remote,
Like a fervid, far word that is told,
It captures the land,
Flung out of the small, throbbing throat;
And the Long Ago is at hand,
The very scent of the mould,
And the look of the bough is the old.

All the stricken go by,
All the years that are trod into dust;
The sad and the blest;   ·
Now Care, with his face from the sky;
Now Sorrow, his head on his breast!
The mood of the Spring — for it must —
As a sword through the sunset is thrust.

Oh my heart and my heart,
When we come to the cold of the year,

The thought of the thrush,
It shall take us and set us apart,
With the low white trees in the hush,
Past the yellowing leaf and the sere, —
Oh my heart, in the cold of the year !

The petals leap up ;
Of a sudden the orchard doth bend,
A room growing bare ;
As out of an emptying cup,
Drips the music out of the air ;
For ghostly the orchard doth bend,
Till the gust and the song are at end !

GROWTH

I CLIMB that was a clod;
  I run whose steps were slow;
I reap the very wheat of God
  That once had none to sow.

Is Joy a lamp outblown?
  Truth out of grasping set?
But nay, for Laughter is mine own;
  I knock and answer get.

Nor is the last word said;
  Nor is the battle done;
Somewhat of glory and of dread
  Remains for set of sun.

For I have scattered seed
  Shall ripen at the end;
Old Age holds more than I shall need,
  Death more than I can spend.

A BELATED ROSE

THE sheaves are gathered in;
The apple-bough is bare;
Whence comes it, lone and rare,
Into this empty air,
Now fast are barn and bin?

What furrow long forgot
Sets here its honeyed sign?
What old seed turns divine? —
Honey enough is mine;
And so I gather not.

The day draws to its close,
The long day and the sore;
And I — I reap no more;
Though at my very door
The harvest is a rose!

RECOMPENSE

OMETIMES, yea, often, I forget,
    forget;
Pass your closed door with not a
    thought of you,
Of the old days, but only of these new;
I sow; I reap; my house in order set.
Then of a sudden doth this thing befall,
By a wood's edge, or in the market-place,
That I remember naught but your dead face,
And other folk forgotten, you are all.
When this is so, oh, sooth the time and
    sweet! —
And I, thereafter, am like unto one
Who from the lilac bloom and the young year
Comes to a chamber shuttered from the street,
Yet heeds nor emptiness nor lack of sun,
For that the recompensing Spring is near!

A CELTIC MAYING SONG

SEVEN candles burn at my love's
　　　head,
　　Seven candles at his feet;
He lies as he were carved of stone
　　Under the winding-sheet.

The Mayers troop into the town
　　Each with a branch of May,
But when they come to my love's house
　　Not one word do they say.

But when they come to my love's house,
　　Silent they stand before ;
Out steps a lad with one white bough,
　　And lays it at the door.

A HOLIDAY

ALONG the pastoral ways I go,
　　To get the healing of the trees;
　　The ghostly news the hedges
　　　　know;
To hive me honey like the bees,
Against the time of snow.

The common hawthorn that I see,
Beside the sunken wall astir,
Or any other blossoming tree,
Is each God's fair white gospeler,
His book upon the knee.

A gust-broken bough; a pilfered nest;
Rumors of orchard or of bin;
The thrifty things of east and west —
The countryside becomes my Inn,
And I its happy Guest.

FIRST LOVE

MY neighbor yonder at her door,
  Looks out and sees the bloom,
Turning the formal Park before
  Into a fair white room.

Of all her life or ill or good,
  This is rememberèd, —
An old house set by an old wood ;
  The lad she did not wed.

CONSOLATION

OH, my belovèd, sweet each hour I
        know
    Because it brings me closer unto
        you!
Boughs make me blithe, and blades give
    comfort true.
When down our sea-worn lanes red leaves drop
    slow,
Soon on the stalk will not the green leaf
    show?
    When blows the crocus as long since it blew,
    Or willows bud by reedy wells we knew —
As went the old, will not the young year go?
Ah, once, drew the dark hour of parting near!
    Each weather was more bitter than the last,
        And fair or sere an added sorrow bore;
But now, belovèd, breaks that time of cheer,
    When I shall see you, hear you, hold you fast,
        And each is sweeter than the one before.

ON A COLONIAL PICTURE

UT of the dusk stepped down
      Young Beauty on the stair;
  What need of April in the town
      When Dolly took the air?

Lilac the color then,
    So all in lilac she;
Her kerchief hid from maids and men
    What was too white to see.

Good Stuart folk her kin,
    And bred in Essex vales;
One looked her happy eyes within,
    And heard the nightingales.

When Dolly took the air,
    Each lad that happened near,
Forgetting all save she was fair,
    Turned English cavalier.

It was the end o' Lent,
 The crocus lit the square ;
With wavering green the bough was bent
 When Dolly took the air.

Long since that weather sped,
 Yet yonder on the wall
Her portrait holds a faded shred,
 Some scrap of it in thrall.

The New World claims the skies,
 Although the Old prevails ;
We look into her happy eyes
 And hear the nightingales.

Staid lilac is her gown,
 And yellow gleams her hair ;
The ghost of April is in town,
 And Dolly takes the air !

A LYRIC ON THE LYRIC

THIS road our blithe-heart elders
   knew,
  And down it trooped together ;
 They plucked their reeds from out
   the dew,
And piped the morning weather.

Shepherd or gallant, cloak or smock,
 They lead where we do follow ;
Hear Colin there among his flock
 To Phyllis in the hollow !

Corinna goes a-Maying yet ;
 Phillida's laugh is ringing ;
And see Castara, violet
 Of early English singing.

But were these lovers never sad,
 Did not some heart go breaking ?

Were youth and cowslips to be had
   Just for the simple taking?

Oh, Sorrow, too, has gone this way,
   And Loss as well as Leisure;
Yet Sorrow lasted for a day,
   And Loss through scarce a measure.

And here Beau Waller stayed to snatch,
   Just at Oblivion's portal,
A single rose that none can match —
   And after grew immortal.

No rain can strip it of its red;
   No gust pelt out its savor;
Though Celia died and he is dead,
   This is the rose he gave her.

What riverside shall grow once more
   The reed bared of dull teaching?
And who shall bring unto our door
   Music instead of preaching?

Yet here forget the evil days;
Let go the Now and After;
Our blithe-heart elders trooped these ways,
And filled them full of Laughter !

DEATH'S GUERDON

SECURE in death he keeps the
    hearts he had ;
Two women have forgot the bitter
    truth ;
To one he is but her sweet little lad ;
To one the husband of her youth.

A MEMORY

THE rosy boughs tossed to the sky ;
   There, as I passed along,
A girl's voice passionate and high
   Rang out in sudden song.

Across the darkening street it came,
   Young, throbbing, sad of fall ;
I think old Homer heard the same
   By some ruined Smyrna wall.

Thereafter, with my memories few,
   That song was a sooth thing ;
Yet went I back no more ; I knew
   That it was gone with Spring.

MYSTERY

ELUDE me still, keep ever just be-
fore,
A cloudy thing, a shape with
wingèd feet.
I shall pursue, but be you strict and fleet,
Unreachable as gusts that pass the door.
Better than doubting eye that eye of yore
Which set tall robbers stalking through the
night;
Or of the wind, lane's hollow, briars white,
Made for the April-tide one ghost the more.
For safe am I that have you still in sight;
See you down each new road, upon you come
In crocus days; under the stripped tree find;
In creed and song, in harvest as in blight;
My chiefest joy till I grow cold and dumb;
Till my years fail, and you are left behind!

KEATS

AN English lad, who, reading in a
book,
A ponderous, leathern thing set
on his knee,
Saw the broad violet of the Egean Sea
Lap at his feet as it were village brook.
Wide was the east; the gusts of morning shook;
Immortal laughter beat along that shore;
Pan crouching in the reeds, piped as of yore;
The gods came down and thundered from that
book.
He lifted his sad eyes; his London street
Swarmed in the sun and strove to make him
heed;
Boys spun their tops, shouting and fair of
cheek:
But still, that violet lapping at his feet, —
An English lad had he sat down to read;
But he rose up and knew himself a Greek.

THE LAVENDER WOMAN

A MARKET SONG

CROOKED, like bough the March
wind bends wallward across
the sleet,
Stands she at her blackened stall
in the loud market street;
All about her in the sun, full-topped, exceeding
sweet,
Lie bundles of gray lavender, a-shrivel in the
heat.

What the Vision that is mine, coming over and
o'er?
'T is the Dorset[1] levels, aye, behind me and
before;
Creeks that slip without a sound from flaggy
shore to shore;
Orchards gnarled with spring-times and as
gust-bound as of yore.

[1] Eastern Shore of Maryland.

Oh, the panes at sunset burning rich-red as the
     rose !
Oh, colonial chimneys that the punctual swal-
     low knows !
Land where like a memory the salt scent stays
     or goes ;
Where wealthy is the reaper and right glad is
     he that sows !

Drips and drips the last June rain, but toward
     the evenfall
Copper gleam the little pools behind the pear-
     trees tall ;
In a whirl of violet, and the fairest thing of all,
The lavender, the lavender sways by the sag-
     ging wall !
.   .   .   .
Fade the levels, the sea-scent, the sheltered
     garden space ;
Town roars all about me, and its roofs are here
     apace ;
Country-sick, with heavy step my homeward
     road I trace
Bearing the keen stuff I bought in the loud
     market-place. ·

Oh, my heart, why should you break at any
    thoughts like these?
So sooth are they of the old time that they
    should bring you ease;
Of Hester in the lavender and out among the
    bees,
Clipping the long stalks one by one under the
    Dorset trees.

RESERVE

KEEP back the one word more,
    Nor give of your whole store ;
    For, it may be, in Art's sole hour
        of need,
Lacking that word, you shall be poor in-
    deed.

OLD AGE

THIS is the hour that just Life sends
    To make amends;
    This closet space where Grief is
        not;
  The World forgot;
And far behind the once-trodden ways
    Enwrapped in haze;
    Here the soft weather fleets
Toward the sun-haunted regions of the West;
    And all about us beats —
As all about a wood stripped of its best,
    A still, prophetic thing —
    The Rumor of the Spring!

A SONG

ALL in an April wood,
　　Met I with Grief;
As I plucked violets
　　And the young leaf.

All in an April wood,
　　Dark Grief I met;
Dark Grief, now I am old,
　　Bides with me yet.

ALL–SAINTS' EVE

H when the ghosts go by,
      Under the empty trees,
   Here in my house I sit and cry,
      My head upon my knees!

Innumerable, white,
   Like mist they fill the square;
The bolt is drawn, the latch made tight,
   The shutter barrèd there.

There walks one small and glad,
   New to the churchyard clod;
My little lad, my little lad,
   A single year with God!

I sit and hide my head
   Until they all are past,
Under the empty trees the dead
   That go full soft and fast.

Up to my chamber dim,
   Back to my bed I plod ;
Oh, would I were a ghost with him,
   And faring back to God !

THE CROCUS

HOW yellow burns the crocus in the
plot !
A little candle-light at a gray wall,
One dauntless moment snatched
from the March brawl,
And like the candle-light to be forgot.
Stripped of the mellower days, the richer lot,
It comes, it goes, an unremembered thing,
And missing all the fullness of the spring,
Thrust from her door, because the time is not.
I am not she you love, but nay, not I !—
I am the crocus which you yonder see,
That, come too soon, although a delicate flower,
Folk turn to praise but go unplucking by;
In love with spring, in love with love, not me,
Pass on and leave me to my little hour !

BLOOM IN AUTUMN

KEEN as though carved against the
mellowing sky,
The orchard lifts before ;
One southward armful blossoming
white and high
Like foam on a sad shore ;
Wraith of his ladhood at an old man's door !

Right glad for it the uncertain, aging Year ;
His straining eyes do see
More than the country levels turning sere ;
More than crooked, quiet tree ;
For back of it his ancient acres be.

He is like one long disinherited,
Who from his ancestral lane,
Sees his lost roofs across the sunset's red,
And, heaped against the pane,
The cherry-boughs he will not pluck again.

There, as he watches, at his feet are blown
The petals torn but fair,
A little of the much that was his own ;
And, for an instant there,
Forgets he all save April in the air !

Remember, too ; but yet, forecasting Age,
Bear you this bough before,
Counting it for your toil enough of wage,
As oft pilgrims of yore
At sight of holy steeples brake and bore

Along the shortening road some blossomed
        thing,
With rapturous shouts and calls,—
So do you with this earnest of that Spring,
Past wavering cheats and thralls,
Whose harvest waits beyond the heavenly walls !

THE LOOK OF THE HEDGE

I WONDER if you know — you who
are gone
So long that you have grown a
mystery —
How Grief at first is such a verity,
He holds us fast from iron dawn to dawn ;
Then, slackening his grasp, he lets us go,
Bearing some littleness of his old mood,
Some odor, sound, some look of fold or
wood, —
You that are gone, I wonder if you know.
This morn the hedge was loosing its spent
white ;
It stung me as with tears.   What thing forgot,
Mixed with this custom of the countryside,
Had happened at some breaking of the light?
The bared briar was rememberèd — but not
This was the very morning that you died !

AT LAST

I THAT was young and had been
warm was dead ;
And, lo ! the beat of boughs upon
the pane !
Then you, groping your way where I had lain
Three stormy sunsets, shrouded foot and
head.
There, leaning me, some choked, low words
you said.
If with such speech your cold lips had been
fain,
In the old time ere living grew so vain,
It would have kept me quick and comforted.
Ah, was it well a longer day to miss,
Shed my sweet youth and of it go denied,
Like stalk of its March bloom, and get but
this ?
This, that you slip a moment to my side,
To pay me for my losses with a kiss ? —
Yea ; in the dark I praised God I had died.

FRA GREGORY'S WORD TO THE LORD

M Y years in this green close are set;
　　The mint buds lilac row by row;
　　Thy suns blaze on; Thy showers
　　　　wet;
And I rejoice that it is so.

Each stalk of lavender is sweet;
　　As I fare back from ailing men,
I smell it out there in the street,
　　And praise Thee I am home again.

Lord, in the shop at Nazareth,
　　Was not the scent of cedar Thine,
Mixed with Thy work a country breath,
　　As is this lavender with mine?

Ever the while I sow or reap,
　　My sick folk seem about me, Lord,

As were I shepherd, they the sheep ;
    Their cares smite through me like a sword.

Fra Simon has a lovely book,
    On rainy days he comes to me,
Over the painted leaves to crook,
    And therefrom read some word of Thee.

Fra Simon wrought this book himself;
    Luke with his viol breaks my heart ;
A few dried simples on a shelf
    Are all my song, and all mine art.

I sort them out on floor and sill ;
    Fennel, and balm, and silver sage ;
This one for fever, this for chill ;
    And, loving each, I get my wage.

Do such as I to glory pass,
    Skilled but in what each season grows ?
I, gatherer of the convent grass,
    With smell of mould about my clothes ?

I cannot sing ; I scarce can pray ;
  Let me have there some garden space,
Where I may dig in mine old way,
  And, looking up, Lord, see Thy face.

A SONG OF THE LAST ROSE

ET me weep the April out ;
(Tears with April come about) ;
Like Ophelia, through the grass
Heavy-headed pass :
For, when Laughter halting goes,
Up my cloudy wits do rear
To the level of the rose,
Last of all the year !

What a heart this handful shows,
Wresting June from out the snows,
June to light a village hedge ;
Getting Youth and vexèd breath —
Youth like gust among the sedge —
At the door of Death !

Flower, at ending of the year,
Up my cloudy wits do rear ;
And I face, as needs I must,
Age as you the dust ;

But I snatch from windy fret,
More than stalk or brier knows;
From this troubled time I get
More than any rose !

LAUGHTER

SPIRIT of the gust and dew,
Herrick had the last of you !
Empty are the morning hills.
Herrick, he whose hearty airs
Still are known in our dull squares ;
Herrick of the daffodils !

He it was in Devon there,
Lad and lover, — a blithe pair, —
Filled his honeyed reed with you ;
Piped the Visions that did pass,
Spring-time through the English grass,
When the thorny hedges blew.

Now the pulpit and the mart
Make an unquiet thing of Art,
For we trade or else we preach ;
Even the crocus, 'stead of song,
Serves for text the April long :
Thus we set it out of reach.

Herrick had the last of you,
Spirit of the gust and dew ! —
Still the ancient Visions pass ;
White of many a blossoming tree,
If we look up, shall we see,
And Corinna in the grass.

A MARSH SONG

FLAGS, and flags, and flags, that,
     blowing, long and slim and
     violet,
Seem like racers, young and myr-
     iad, all behind me and before,
Running, leaping, fast beside me, with their
     faces townward set;
And my heart is glad to see them, and I laugh
     out as of yore.

Now the willows rock and rock against the
     thin gold of the sky!
Now a star is there above them, beaten out
     upon the gold:
But the flags are straining forward, bending
     low and straightening high,
And the air has caught the sea-tang that the
     darkening levels hold.

Ellen is a bramble-blossom foaming white on
    thorny stalk,
Melting out some hedge's hollow like the snow
    of Candlemas ;
Margaret is soft and willful, and she minds me,
    in her talk,
Of the blackbird's hearty whistle when the
    orchards brim with grass.

Oh, I love not, and I care not, and I let the
    maids pass by ;
Yet I know one at her house-door sitting with
    her head bent low,
And her gown is like the marsh-buds, and of
    violet is her eye,
And the flags are leaping, leaping, as they
    point the way to go !

Cambridge town and Cambridge town is scarce
    a mile across the wind,
And it keeps her and it holds her past the
    purpling of the reeds ;

If Love waits me on the highway, if Love
    plucks me and is kind,
What can any lad do better than to follow
    where he leads ?

Now the masts rise up before me as a far and
    empty wood ;
From the east lands and the west lands come
    the great stars one by one ;
Now the willows rock and vanish with the
    odors keen and good ;
Now the flags are mist behind me, and the
    racing is all done !